HOW

TO FEED A

VEGETARIAN

HELP FOR
NON-VEGETARIAN COOKS

Suzanne D'Avalon

Published by

P L A C I D L Y

A m I d t h e N o I s e
P.O. Box 16914
Colorado Springs, CO
80935-6914

Printed in the United States of America

Library of Congress Cataloging in Publication Data

D'Avalon, Suzanne P.
  How to feed a vegetarian: help for non-vegetarian
  cooks.
  p. cm.
  ISBN 0-9650941-0-3
  1. Vegetarian cookery   2. Cookery, American
  I. Title
TX837.D245H
                                        96-67110
                                           CIP

"Go placidly amid the noise and the haste,
and remember what peace there may be in silence"

From the DESIDERATA
by Max Ehrmann

ACKNOWLEDGMENTS

If I had known how much work this book would be, I probably would have never started. However, I did start and was amazed at the doors that opened along the way.

Many thanks to:

Bruce Grodnik ("UncleMicro") and his unending patience with the less technically endowed.

Diane King and Sonia Weiss, who magically appeared at the moment I needed proofreaders and editing advice.

The Colorado Independent Publishers Association and the Publishers Marketing Association, whose members patiently answered my many questions.

The enthusiastic friends - Gerda, Abby, DeAnn, Karen, and Hunter - for their encouragement.

Thank you all!

Plac. Amid 1

CONTENTS

CONTENTS

(continued)

This book is made with OTABIND. To lay flat, open the book to the desired page. Either bend the pages backward, or press along the inside crease where the page attaches to the spine.

Dear Cook,

My story is pretty simple. I became a vegetarian four years ago, primarily because I felt tired of always feeling tired. Within weeks my strength and energy increased, so I stuck with it.

In the course of learning to feed myself all over again at the age of 37, I learned about nutrition, about cooking methods, about foods I didn't know existed, and about the hidden sources of animal products.

My reason for writing this cookbook is also simple. I believe it was after the third invitation to stay for dinner, when the hostess said, "We're having chicken stir-fry, but you can pick the chicken out." At that point I decided I could provide a benefit to society, that I could provide a gentle guide to vegetarians and the foods they eat which is designed specifically for the non-vegetarian cook.

I like to eat. I also really like it when someone else cooks for me. So I admit, I wrote this book out of a sense of self-preservation. And I do want you to enjoy yourself as well, when you invite me over for dinner.

Suzanne D'Avalon

A CHANGING SOCIETY

Vegetarians used to be those long-haired hippies of the 1960's. No longer. A 1992 survey estimates that almost 13 million Americans, 7% of the population, are vegetarian, and the ranks are growing. Sooner or later, one's going to appear in your life.

Regardless of what they call themselves, more people are preferring to eat vegetarian meals. A 1991 Gallup poll for the National Restaurant Association revealed that 20% of the American population looks for a vegetarian menu when eating out, and up to a third orders vegetarian fare if listed on the menu. And that was a few years ago.

Finally, take a look at the increase in non-meat products on the supermarket shelves and in the frozen food sections, especially if it's labeled "low fat." Lot more variety of meat-less soups and frozen entrees, as well as increased aisle space devoted to "health food."

The good news about these increasing vegetarian preferences? You have this book to help you!

DISCLAIMER

This book is designed to provide information in regard to the subject matter covered. It is sold with the understanding that the publisher and author are not engaged in providing dietary or medical services. If such assistance is required, the services of a competent professional should be sought.

The purpose of this book is to educate and entertain. The author and PLACIDLY AMID THE NOISE shall have neither liability nor responsibility to any person or entity with respect to any loss or damage caused or alleged to be caused directly or indirectly by the information contained in this book.

THE BEGINNING

This book is written for the non-vegetarian cook who wants to prepare a meal that will please and satisfy a vegetarian guest. The assumption is that the cook is not totally familiar with vegetarian ingredients.

By preparing a meal, I mean more effort than adding water to a prepackaged mix. However, this is not gourmet cooking! The recipes are for 'real' food that have been kitchen tested.

If you have a vegetarian in the household, I urge you to invest in a proper vegetarian cookbook. You'll use it. See PAGE 111 for suggestions.

RECIPES WERE SELECTED ON THE BASIS OF INGREDIENTS BEING AVAILABLE AT SUPERMARKETS. For those of you concerned about your reputations, you need never be seen in a health food store.

One way to look at a vegetarian diet, especially if imposed for health reasons, is the same as looking at a half a glass of water. Depending on your perspective, the glass is either half empty or half full. Likewise, eating can become pleasureless if only looking at the foods not available. Instead, look at the wide variety of vegetarian ingredients that are available. See PAGE 109 for a view of the possible.

The key to great tasting vegetarian food is nothing new. Use fresh ingredients as much as possible, and avoid over-cooking.

So, good luck!

Oh, and enjoy yourself along the way.

Abbreviations Used

tsp   = teaspoon

TBLS = tablespoon

oz   = ounce

lb   = pound

DID YOU KNOW....

The term "vegetarian" was first used in 1847 in England. The occasion was the inaugural meeting of the Vegetarian Society of the United Kingdom, held on September 30 by Joseph Brotherton at Northwood Villa in Kent, England.

The word was derived from the Latin "vegetus," meaning whole, sound, fresh, and lively. It is not to be confused with the term "vegetable-arian," a mythical human that supposedly subsists entirely on only vegetables.

The correct pronuncation of 'vegetarian' is

vej - i - tár - ē - en

and not,

vej - i - tér - e - bel

Please make a note of it!

TYPES OF VEGETARIANS

Vegetarians now come in many variations as to what they will or will not eat. Asking a few questions before planning your dinner menu will insure that everyone enjoys your slaving over a hot stove. The vegetarian in particular will think you're a very thoughtful person.

VEGETARIAN: basically, no meat! No beef, no pork, no chicken, no fish. Nor any of the broth used in preparing these foods. And no lard. Yes, chicken and fish are considered meat, because they came from life forms that used to move about until they were killed and gutted. No, it's not very polite at all to fix a chicken stew and tell your guest, "well, you can pick out the chicken." If you are serving meat, prepare it separately from the rest of the dishes.

"Vegetarian" has become a loosely defined term in recent years. To be on the safe side, do not serve dairy products, eggs, or gelatin. For egg-free, avoid mayonnaise, check labels, and use EGG REPLACER in any baking. Do not use EGG BEATERS or egg replacement products found next to the eggs in the dairy section -- these are NOT egg free products. No dairy means no milk, no cheese, no sour cream, no butter, no product with "whey" or "lactose" in the list of ingredients. Instead, use soy milk or rice milk, canola margarine, and tofu. Avoid gelatin, unless you know how strict your guest's diet is. Gelatin is made from the hooves of cows and horses.

OVO-VEGETARIAN: While not eating meat or dairy, Ovo-Vegetarians do eat eggs.

LACTO-VEGETARIAN: While not eating meat or eggs, Lacto-Vegetarians do ingest dairy products.

OVO-LACTO-VEGETARIAN: Yes, you guessed it. Doesn't eat meat, but does eat eggs and dairy. This is probably the most common type of vegetarian you'll meet.

VEGANS: Vegans eat no animal products at all. In addition to no meat (causing the death of an animal), and no dairy (taken from living cows), they eat no food product associated with an animal. This means no honey, no eggs, no gelatin. These folks are the strictest.

FREQUENT GUEST CHECKLIST

If a vegetarian diet is not your normal mode of eating, you'll probably lose track of what your guests do not eat. Make it easy on yourself. Ask them once, and mark their responses on the opposite page.

Asking before hand is not rude, and if anything, indicates a desire on your part to make your guest feel comfortable and welcome. You may also save wear and tear on yourself, because you'll no longer need to spend time worrying about whether your lunch or dinner menu is acceptable.

__GUESTS__

DOES **NOT** EAT	/	/	/	/
Red meat				
Poultry				
Fish				
Eggs				
Milk Products				
Cheese				
Other Dairy				
Honey				
Gelatin				
OTHER				

WHY DO THEY DO THAT?

There are lots of reasons why people choose a vegetarian lifestyle. I'll list a few, and feel free to ask your guests their specific reasons.

1) Dietary & Health

Vegetarian diets are generally lower in fat overall, and emphasize freshly prepared vegetables and grains. People may start out on a vegetarian diet because they need to lose weight or because of gastro-intestinal irritations.

Then there are those pesky medical studies that show vegetarians as a group have lower blood pressure, lower rates of diabetes, longer life spans, less incidence of hypertension, lung cancer, osteoporosis, kidney stones, and gallstones, better calcium absorption, less risk of obesity, less incidence of PMS, and lower mortality rates from chronic degenerative diseases.

2) Food Allergies

Some symptoms of food allergies include headaches, hypoglycemia, excessively swelled stomach, nausea or tiredness after eating, palpitations, sweating, mental fuzziness after eating, skin rashes, ringing in the ears, diarrhea, constipation, and nasal congestion. For instance, MSG may cause headaches.   Dairy products promote the forming of mucous in the body, which may lead to sinus congestion and headaches.   Lacto intolerant people often react to dairy products with diarrhea and intestinal distress.

More knowledge is being gained about chemical allergies, and people reacting to the pesticides and hormones used to raise food commercially. Organically grown vegetables are becoming pretty easy to buy in health food stores, although still hard to find in supermarkets.

Organically raised meat is not too easy to find or verify. First, 55% of the antibiotics in the US are fed to livestock. Second, it's difficult to trace what was put in the soil or sprayed on the fodder before it even got to the cows. Whatever chemicals the cows ingest will then find their way into the stomachs and bodies of whoever ingests the cow.

3) Ecological

Grains produce five times more protein per acre than livestock. Beans produce 10 times more protein per acre than livestock.

33% of all raw materials consumed in the US are used in the production of meat and dairy.

2,500 gallons of water are needed to produce 1 pound of meat, while 25 gallons are needed to produce 1 pound of wheat. In addition, The production and processing of livestock depletes 20 million acre-feet of ground water annually.

About 60 million people could be fed by the grain given to livestock if Americans reduced their meat diet by as little as 10%. 800 million people could be saved from starvation on the grains and legumes used to feed livestock.

Meat diets are not very healthy for Mother Earth.

4) Humanitarian

Some people believe, especially in this age of rapid transit and technology, that there is no need for an animal to die in order for them to live. We're no longer a hunter society.

The largest source of cruelty to animals is farms. Cows may have their tails cut off for the convenience of the milking machine. Chickens may never live outside a tiny cubicle. Calves may never stand on their own feet while harnessed in stalls, being fattened for early slaughter.

5) Joining the Club

Some people might become vegetarian because they want to be associated with other famous vegetarians, such as Leonardo Da Vinci, Benjamin Franklin, Albert Einstein, Buddha, George Bernard Shaw, Socrates, Plato, St. Francis of Assisi, Star Trek's Mr. Spock from the planet Vulcan (the entire planet is vegetarian!), basketball player Bill Walton, Brigit Bardot, Raquel Welch, and Clint Eastwood.

GUIDE TO WEIRD FOOD

Some of the foods found regularly in a vegetarian diet may not be known in your own diet. Here's a brief introduction to some of those "weird foods", and where you may find them in the supermarket aisles. A personal tour of the four supermarket chains in my area found that three of the four stores carried all the items listed below. The fourth store, a no-frills warehouse type operation, carried only some of the items.

VEGETABLE BROTH -- comes in jars or cubes. Use the same as meat-based broth, a teaspoon in a cup of boiling water. Can be found in "SOUPS," "HEALTH FOOD," or "DIETETIC."

SOY MILK OR RICE MILK -- comes in pint and quart containers, made of cardboard. Does not need refrigeration until opened. Generally this product can sit around on your shelves for months before being used. Can be found in "HEALTH FOOD" or "DIETETIC."

TOFU -- compressed white cake made from bean curd, coming in three varieties, hard, soft, and silken. Needs to be refrigerated and used within a few days. Usually found in

"DAIRY" or "PRODUCE." (See PAGE 52 for more information on tofu.)

TAMARI SAUCE OR SOY SAUCE -- a basic seasoning liquid made from soy beans. Tamari sauce is usually wheat-free, and somewhat less salty than soy sauce. Both types come in low-sodium varieties. Look in "ORIENTAL," "HEALTH FOOD," or "DIETETIC."

BASMATI RICE -- a long grain white rice with a sweet nutty flavor. Look in "RICE & PASTA" or "HEALTH FOOD."

BROWN RICE -- the most nutritious of all rice because the outer layer of bran is left intact. Look in "RICE & PASTA" or "HEALTH FOOD."

LENTILS -- a dried legume that does not require pre-soaking, cooks quickly, and is very versatile. Comes in green and red. The red variety is smaller, cooks faster, actually looks more orangish than reddish, and turns yellow when cooked. Can be used interchangeably. Should be easy to find among the "DRIED BEANS." If not, try "HEALTH FOOD."

RICE STICKS OR RICE NOODLES -- a noodle made of rice! Looks like hard white threads in the package and becomes semi-transparent when cooked, which only takes 5 minutes or less. Look for them in the "ORIENTAL FOOD" aisle, in a cellophane package. Read the package label carefully for the words "rice sticks." There is a similar package of noodles called "cellophane noodles," which are made from mung beans and potato starch. Initially, the non-vegetarian eater (presumably you) will probably enjoy the rice variety more.

HEALTH FOOD STORES

If you do visit a health food store, take a look at the different kinds of rice and beans. Far more variety than you'll find in the grocery store, plus usually the options to buy organic or to buy in bulk (which means you can purchase as little as you need).

While you're there, stock up on vegetable broth (it's much cheaper in bulk), and pick up a box of EGG REPLACER (made by ENER-G Foods), a powder replacement for eggs that when mixed with water can be substituted in all your recipes. Although not used in this cookbook, EGG REPLACER is a very handy item to have in the house, especially if you think you want to feed the vegetarian again sometime. Remember, products advertised as egg replacements in supermarkets often are made from eggs, and therefore not suitable if your guest doesn't eat eggs.

ORIENTAL MARKETS

All of the above weird food is also generally available in oriental food stores and markets. I prefer to buy my rice in bulk at these stores, as I find the price is usually less.

Again, the meat diet in the United States is a cultural habit. Visiting an oriental market can be a short excursion into another culture. Browse the shelves or ask for specifics. In either case, explore and have fun!

STOCKING UP

One of my habits is to do grocery shopping at night, the later the better, after the hordes are no longer in the aisles. So I usually stock my pantry with frequent use items in order to cut down on the trips to the supermarket. In case you do the same, here is a list of non-perishable ingredients used in this cookbook for you to consider stocking in advance:

- ✓ Vegetable Broth
- ✓ Soy or Rice Milk
- ✓ Tamari or Soy Sauce
- ✓ Basmati Rice
- ✓ Brown Rice
- ✓ Sesame Oil
- ✓ Rice Sticks
- ✓ Dried lentils, red or green
- ✓ Dried or canned beans:
     black, pinto, navy, kidney

You'll need to buy TOFU fresh whenever you want to use it. Other ingredients used in this cookbook are listed on the HALF FULL VIEW on PAGE 108.

HOW TO

HOW TO ROAST RED PEPPERS

Preheat oven to 400° F. Place peppers on cookie sheet and put into oven on lowest rack. The pepper skins will bubble up and slightly blacken in places. Turn frequently, until all sides are roasted and mostly puffy. Depending on your oven, this process will take anywhere from 15 to 30 minutes. Remove peppers from oven and place immediately into a paper bag. Close the bag, and let set for at least 15 minutes. Longer is fine. When the peppers are cool, peel the skins, and remove the membranes and seeds. Then you may slice, chop, or dice as your recipe instructs.

HOW TO MAKE OAT CRUMBS

I've given up using bread crumbs, for several reasons. First, oats are a water soluble fiber. Wheat is not. Water soluble fibers such as oats are simply easier for the body to digest. Second, making oat crumbs is cheaper than buying bread crumbs. To make oat crumbs, place rolled oats into a nut grinder or the grinding mechanism of your food processor. The results are generally one for one, meaning that a half cup of rolled oats will yield a half cup of oat crumbs.

TIPS ON SEASONINGS

As people change to vegetarian diets, they often become more knowledgeable about food, and make changes not related to vegetables and meats. Just like we all know that a lot of the potato's nutrition is in the potato skin, many vegetarians know this also applies in other foods such as rice, wheat, and sugar.

White flour is made from wheat where the outer layer called the bran has been removed. Same for processed white rice and granulated sugar. To gain back the nutrition lost in the food factories, vegetarians make a few other changes. Honey, maple syrup, molasses, and fructose are substituted for sugar. Whole grain flour is used in place of the white stuff. Brown rice replaces the quick-cooking converted kind. The use of oils is changed to sautéing and braising instead of frying, and to polyunsaturated fats found in olive and canola oils.

As the diet changes, the palate, one's desire for certain tastes, also changes. Which is why the vegetarian diet can initially seem bland to the non-vegetarian, until the palate adapts (usually a process of weeks to a couple of months). Typical American diets are high in salt, sugar, and fats. Vegetarian diets are not (yet) the typical American diet. A person expecting the surges and rushes associated with eating sugar, salt, and fat can feel disappointed by vegetarian food.

So here are the tips...

1) Follow the seasonings as listed in the recipes, at least initially. If adapting your own recipes, consider erring on the side of less salt, oil, and sugar. Use a salt-substitute seasoning or all herbal seasoning for a stronger flavoring without the salt or sugar.

2) Set a condiments tray on the table which can include any of the following: salt and pepper, sugar bowl, honey pot, maple syrup, ketchup, spicy mustard, lemon slices, tamari sauce, butter, canola margarine, fructose bowl (fructose is a sweetener made from fruit; it comes in a white granulated form, and can be found usually in the "DIETETIC" aisle), or whatever else you wish.

Let everyone, including yourself, season as he or she desires.

SALADS

NOTES:

The salad recipes are substantial, meaning the salads are filling. They work nicely at luncheon, buffets, or light suppers served with soup and side dishes. Salad greens are great with main dishes, but generally have insufficient nutrition to satisfy hunger.

When using salad greens, the darker the leaf the better. Consider using romaine, bibb, boston, or leaf lettuce. Try substituting a spinach or cabbage salad. Unless it's a very small part of a large meal, try to avoid iceberg lettuce. While iceberg lettuce is indeed popular for its crunch and keeping ability, it is also 90% water and therefore provides very little to fuel the body. At a minimum, mix in other greens with iceberg lettuce.

THE OTHER BEAN SALAD

3/4 cup black turtle beans

3/4 cup pinto beans

3/4 cup navy beans

1 medium sweet onion (such as Vidalia)

1/4 cup cider vinegar

2 tsps sugar

1/2 tsp salt

1 yellow bell pepper, roasted and diced (see PAGE 29)

1 red bell pepper, roasted and diced (see PAGE 29)

1/2 cup black olives, chopped

3 TBLS fresh cilantro, chopped

1/2 cup Herbed Vinaigrette dressing

salt, pepper

◆ Prepare beans in separate containers and pans, as cooking times vary. Soak beans overnight and drain. Place in separate pans, cover with water, bring to a boil, and then reduce to simmer, for 45 minutes to an hour, until beans are soft. Rinse and drain, and mix together in large bowl. Let stand or refrigerate until cool.

◆ Slice the onion as thin as possible. Combine vinegar, sugar, and salt in a bowl. Add the onion slices. Stir until the onions are well coated. Set aside.

◆ Mix together: beans, drained onion, peppers, olives, and cilantro. Toss with 1/2 cup of vinaigrette dressing. Salt and pepper to taste, if desired.

◆ Serve with croutons. Optional serving suggestion: toss lettuce leaves in dressing, arrange on a platter; place bean mixture on top and add croutons. Serves 6 to 8.

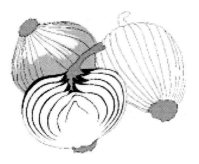

NOTES: If you want a milder onion flavor or can't find a sweet onion, then make the onion mixture the night before and let it marinade for 24 hours. For a faster bean approach, use one 16 oz can each of black, pinto, and navy beans, <u>thoroughly</u> rinsed and drained.

EARTH SALAD

4 medium carrots, scrubbed or peeled

1 parsnip, scrubbed or peeled

2 small beetroots, scrubbed or peeled

1 small celeriac root, peeled

Tamari Vinaigrette dressing, to coat

◆ Grate the above roots. Easiest way: feed everything through the large hole grater on the food processor.

◆ Combine all grated roots in a bowl. Toss with Tamari Vinaigrette dressing, or a vinaigrette dressing of choice. Serves 6.

> **NOTES:** You <u>must</u> use fresh, raw beets. Canned will not do! Celeriac root is usually available amongst the specialty vegetables in the produce section. The flavor is great and blends well in this salad. If you can't find it, then use 2 stalks of celery, finely sliced, or 1/2 rutabaga, grated. Celery and celeriac root are two entirely separate plants! If the vegetables are organic, then scrubbing is fine, otherwise peel.

RICE & LENTIL SALAD

1 1/2 cups red lentils, rinsed and drained

3 cups water

1 cup cooked basmati or white rice

1 green pepper, chopped

1 small onion, chopped fine

1 stalk celery, chopped

2 TBLS pimento-stuffed green olives, sliced

1 tsp salt

1/2 cup Italian or vinaigrette salad dressing

◆ Bring lentils to boil in the 3 cups of water in a covered pan. Reduce heat, and simmer for 20 minutes until the lentils are tender. Drain.

◆ Combine remaining ingredients in a bowl. Add the drained lentils. Mix well, and chill until ready to serve. Serves 6 to 8.

NOTES: For a sweeter taste, use one roasted, peeled, and chopped red pepper instead of the green. My quick salad dressing is Newman's Own, because it leaves out the chemicals and additives, and I like having the profits go to charity. If you really like tomatoes, reduce the green pepper and onion, and add one small diced tomato.

MARINATED SLAW

2 cups cabbage shredded (about 1/2 small head)

1 red pepper, roasted and diced (see PAGE 29)

1 medium to large carrot, shredded

1/2 cucumber, chopped

1 sweet onion, finely sliced (optional)

1 cup fresh spinach, shredded

3 TBLS honey

1 TBLS cold water

2 TBLS red wine vinegar

1 TBLS white vinegar

2 TBLS vegetable oil

1 tsp salt

1 clove minced garlic or 1/4 tsp garlic granules

◆   Chop, shred, and dice cabbage, red pepper, carrot, cucumber, onion and spinach.   Combine all together in large bowl.

◆   Combine honey, water, vinegars, oil, salt, and garlic in blender. Pour over vegetables and toss to coat. Let sit for several hours or overnight in refrigerator. Serves 6.

NOTES: Substitute 1/2 diced green pepper for the roasted red pepper, if you wish. This salad also tastes great without the onion. But if you do want a very sweet or mild onion flavor, follow the instructions for marinating an onion under "THE OTHER BEAN SALAD" on PAGE 34.

CHEATER'S SPECIALTY

Add 1/2 tsp to 1 tsp prepared dijon mustard to a half cup of vinaigrette or Italian dressing. Vary the proportion to your taste. A stronger mustard flavor goes nicely over raw shredded red cabbage. A milder mustard flavor could be used with Earth Salad

FRESH SLAW

2 cups cabbage, finely chopped

3/4 cup carrot, grated

1/2 cup green pepper, chopped (optional)

1/2 cup cucumber, chopped (optional)

3 TBLS vinegar

2 TBLS vegetable oil

1/4 tsp dry mustard

1 TBLS sugar or 1/2 TBLS honey

◆   Chop or grate cabbage, carrot, green pepper, and cucumber, either by hand or with a food processor. Combine all together in a large bowl.

◆ Combine vinegar, oil, mustard and sweetener. Toss with vegetables to coat. Serves 4 to 6.

HERBED VINAIGRETTE DRESSING

1/2 cup olive oil

1/2 cup water

1 1/2 TBLS red wine vinegar

1 1/2 TBLS balsamic vinegar

1/2 tsp each of cilantro, thyme, basil, and salt

1/4 tsp each of sage and ground cumin

1 tsp each of honey and prepared mustard

1/2 tsp garlic granules or powder

black pepper to taste

◆ Mix all together in a blender or food processor. Makes about 1 cup.

NOTES: In the interest of reducing fat content, I often use part oil and part water in a salad dressing. If you like a more full bodied dressing, substitute 1/2 cup of vegetable oil for the water.

TAMARI VINAIGRETTE DRESSING

3/4 cup olive or sunflower seed oil

1/4 cup plus 2 TBLS cider vinegar

1 tsp honey

2 tsps tamari or soy sauce

1 pea-size piece of fresh ginger, grated

1/4 tsp rosemary

1 whole clove garlic, peeled

◆ Mix all ingredients, except for garlic, together in a blender or food processor.

◆ Pour into a bottle or glass jar, and add the whole garlic clove. For fullest flavor, let sit for a couple days before use. Makes about 1 cup.

NOTES: For a lighter dressing, reduce oil to 1/2 cup and add 1/4 cup of water. You may substitute 1/4 tsp garlic granules and 1/8 tsp ginger if fresh garlic and ginger are not available.

SOUPS

NOTES:

Soup recipes can be fairly easy to adapt to vegetarian needs. Substitute vegetable broth for meat-based broth.

SCRATCH BROTH

2 1/2 to 3 quarts of water

2 onions

1 zucchini

4 cloves garlic

4 carrots

4 celery stalks

1 parsnip

1 turnip

1 bunch parsley

1/2 tsp each thyme, dried basil, and salt

1 bay leaf

2 peppercorns

◆ Chop all vegetables, and place into large pot with water. Add herbs. Bring to a boil, cover, reduce heat, and simmer for 2 to 3 hours.

◆ Place a double layer of cheesecloth inside a colander. Set the colander over a large bowl or pot, that will catch the broth as it flows through the cheesecloth and colander. Pour in the contents of the cooking pot. Gather up the edges of the cheese cloth, and squeeze the remaining liquid from the vegetables. Yields about 10 cups of broth.

SWEET & SOUR BORSCHT

3 medium beets, with tops

2 TBLS olive oil

1 onion, chopped

3 carrots, sliced

2 cups cabbage, coarsely shredded

2 lemons, squeezed (about 1/4 cup of juice)

3 TBLS brown sugar or 2 TBLS honey

1 tsp dill weed

6 cups vegetable stock

◆ Prepare the beets by cutting off the tops and discarding stems and wilted leaves. Wash remaining leaves, and chop coarsely. Set aside. Wash the beets to remove excess dirt, peel, and coarsely shred.

◆ Heat oil in large pan over medium heat. Add onion and carrots. Cook about 10 minutes, until soft, stirring occasionally. Add beets, tops, cabbage, lemon juice, sweetener, dill, and stock. Bring to a simmer. Reduce heat, cover and simmer until beets and cabbage are tender, about 45 minutes. Salt and pepper to taste. Serves 6.

NOTES: For a chunkier soup, coarsely chop or slice the cabbage instead of shredding. If your guests eat dairy, garnish with sour cream or plain yogurt.

AZTEC SOUP

2 TBLS olive oil

1 large onion, coarsely chopped

2 cloves garlic, minced

12 cups vegetable stock

4 cups butternut or hubbard squash, peeled and diced

2 10 oz packages of frozen corn

PART I: THE SOUP

◆ Sauté onion and garlic in olive oil until onion is golden. Add stock and squash, bringing to a boil. Reduce heat, cover, and simmer until tender, about 10 to 15 minutes.

◆ Add corn, and cook additional 5 minutes. Salt and pepper to taste. Serve with a variety of condiments, as shown in **PART II**. Each person creates a soup to his or her own tastes. Serves 8 to 10.

PART II: THE CONDIMENTS

◆ Pick your favorites below and place them in small bowls on the serving table.   Each guest then adds condiments to his or her bowl of soup.

Avocado -- peeled and diced

Tortilla chips -- the 100% white corn ones are most excellent

Cheese -- 1 to 3 cups of shredded jack cheese or soy cheese

Roasted nuts -- melt 1 TBLS canola margarine over medium heat.   Add 3/4 cup of walnut halves and 2/3 cup pine nuts. Stir and cook until golden, about 2 minutes.

Seeds -- toasted shelled pumpkin seeds, if you can find them, otherwise roasted   shelled sunflower seeds are good. For something special, place raw sunflower seeds in a frying pan, heating until brown; add a dash or two of tamari sauce, stir quickly, and remove from heat.

Peppers -- roasted green chili peppers (comes in cans), or roasted and diced red bell pepper.

NOTES: The work is in the cutting and slicing of ingredients. The soup itself is pretty fast to fix. And it's fun to eat.

WHITE BEAN & GARLIC CHOWDER

1 1/2 cups navy beans, soaked overnight, rinsed, and drained

8 cups vegetable stock

bouquet garni (see below)

1 whole bulb garlic, separated into cloves and peeled

1 large diced potato (about 1 cup)

2 TBLS olive oil

1 onion, chopped

2 carrots, thinly sliced (about 1 cup)

salt, pepper

1 cup chopped fresh parsley

1 cup soy, rice, or almond milk

◆ Make bouquet garni by placing the following in a scrap of cheese cloth: 1/2 to 1 tsp rosemary, 1 tsp thyme, 1/2 tsp whole fennel seeds, 1 bay leaf, 4 whole cloves. Tie the cheese cloth into a bundle.

◆ Place beans in a large pot with 4 cups of stock; add garlic and bouquet garni. Cover and simmer 1 hour. Add potato, and simmer another 1/2 hour. Beans should now be soft. If not, continue to simmer until soft.

◆ In separate pan, sauté onions in olive oil until translucent. Add carrots, and sauté until carrots are crisp tender (mostly cooked for still having a bit of a crunch when eaten).

◆ Add carrots and onions to soup pan, along with remaining 4 cups of stock. Simmer 15 to 20 minutes.

◆ Remove the bouquet garni. Puree 1/2 the soup in a blender or food processor until smooth. Stir the puree back into the soup, and reheat. Add salt and pepper to taste. Add milk and parsley, and serve. Serves 8.

NOTES: The milk is optional, but does add some extra creaminess. If available in the supermarket, almond milk is more flavorful than soy milk. When pureeing half the mixture, I take the time to pick out the whole garlic cloves in the half to be pureed. The garlic becomes pretty mellow after simmering so long, but I'd still rather not bite into a whole clove.

CREAM OF WALNUT SOUP

1 1/2 cups coarsely chopped walnuts

water

2 cups soy or rice milk

1/2 bay leaf

1/4 tsp each thyme and basil

2 TBLS chopped parsley

2 TBLS olive oil

1 large stalk celery, thinly sliced

1 medium onion, diced

2 TBLS whole wheat flour

3 cups vegetable stock

2 TBLS dry sherry

salt, pepper

finely chopped chives or green onion

◆ In a pan over medium heat, cover walnuts with water and bring to a boil. Boil for 3 minutes. Drain, rinse with cold water, and drain again. Pour milk over drained nuts, and add bay leaf, thyme, basil, and parsley. Heat to scalding. Cover, remove from heat, and let sit for 20 minutes.

◆ Heat olive oil in 3 quart pan over medium heat. Add onion and celery, cooking and stirring for 5 minutes. Stir in flour and cook 1 more minute. Gradually stir in stock, cooking and stirring until soup boils. Reduce heat and simmer for 10 minutes.

◆ Remove the bay leaf from the milk-nut mixture; add milk-nut mixture to soup pan. Puree all the soup in a blender or food processor. Return to pan and stir in sherry. Add salt and pepper to taste. Gently reheat, without boiling. Garnish with chives or green onion, if desired. Serves 6 to 8.

NOTES: For a richer soup, use almond milk. You may wish to experiment with fresh herbs in this recipe. Substitute 1 tablespoon of fresh for each 1/2 teaspoon of dried.

HOW

TO BE FRIENDS

WITH TOFU

Tofu. Maligned and jeered in the Western world. And not a pretty sight either. A whitish-gray brick that looks unappetizing, and is in fact rather tasteless. Made from soy beans, it's a product that first appeared 2000 years ago in China. And yes, tofu is "real" food.

From a nutritional standpoint, tofu is wonderful because it is a complete protein, without the cholesterol and saturated fat. From a cooking standpoint, it absorbs the flavors of whatever it is combined with, and makes an excellent filler. And from the subterfuge standpoint, often meat eaters won't know "that tofu stuff" is in there unless you tell them.

Tofu comes in three types: silken, soft, and hard (also sometimes called firm). Silken is used primarily in sauces. Soft tofu is used mainly in baking and pies. Firm tofu is most often used in loaves, casseroles, and main dishes. The recipes in this book primarily call for firm tofu.

Tofu can be used in recipes in three ways: 1)AS IS, 2) BAKED, or 3) FROZEN AND THAWED.

1) AS IS

Firm tofu, used straight from the package, will break up during cooking, becoming small pieces like cottage cheese. Wrap the tofu in a towel and let sit for 10 minutes before using. If you want minuscule pieces, cream the tofu in the food processor before using in Chili or No Meat Loaf.

2) BAKED

Baking is a way to "toughen up" tofu to hold its shape. Begin the same as above, wrapping the tofu in a towel and let sit for 10 minutes. Cut into 1/2 inch slices, place on a cookie sheet in the oven at 350° F for 20 to 30 minutes, turning once halfway through.

3) FROZEN AND THAWED

Tofu changes its texture once its been frozen, again making it hold together in recipes. Stick the whole package in the freezer. Once it's frozen, take it out and let it thaw. After it's thawed, drain and literally wring out the water. Wrap a towel around the tofu and let it sit for 10 minutes. Then cut or slice and add to your recipe.

MAIN DISHES

NOTES:

All of these selections should also satisfy the meat eater, so you do not need to be cooking two meals at once.

The recipes listed above with an asterisk (*) indicate recipes that can easily be made hours or days in advance, and set aside until cooking time.

RICE & CARROT LOAF

1/2 cup peanut butter

1 cup soy or rice milk

2 TBLS olive oil

1 small onion, minced

1/2 tsp salt

1/4 tsp sage

1/2 cup oat crumbs (see PAGE 29)

2 cups carrots, grated

1 cup cooked brown rice

1/2 cup coarsely ground walnuts (optional)

◆ Cream together peanut butter and milk. Set aside.

◆ Sauté onion in olive oil until soft. Add salt, sage, and oat crumbs. Sauté for 2 more minutes. Remove from heat.

◆ Add peanut butter mixture to onions. Stir in rice, grated carrots, and walnuts. Press into oiled casserole dish or loaf pan. Bake at 350° F for about an hour. Serves 4 to 6.

> **NOTES:** This is a great dish for leftover rice, and other rice besides brown rice could be substituted. If you're not a peanut butter fan, substitute SESAME TAHINI, a thick nut butter made from sesame seeds instead of peanuts. Look for it in a glass jar in the 'HEALTH FOOD' aisle.

STUFFED PEPPERS

4 large red or green peppers

1 TBLS olive oil

1 medium onion, chopped

2 stalks celery, diced

1 1/2 tsp cumin

1 1/2 tsp chili powder

1 1/2 tsp basil

1 tsp oregano

1   15 oz can of kidney beans

2 cups cooked brown rice

2 TBLS tamari sauce

cayenne pepper

1   15 oz can of tomato sauce

◆   Preheat oven to 350° F.

◆   Wash the peppers, cut in half lengthwise, and remove seeds.   Place cut side down in a single layer on a vegetable steamer over boiling water.   Cover and steam until just starting to get soft, about 10 minutes.   You may have to do this in two batches.

◆ Heat olive oil in a skillet. Add onions, celery, cumin, chili powder, basil, and oregano. Sauté until the onions are almost soft. Remove from heat.

◆ Drain and rinse the kidney beans. Add the beans and rice to the onions, and mix. Add the tamari sauce, and for extra zest, add a bit of cayenne pepper to taste. Mix again.

◆ Fill each pepper with rice mixture, and place in a lightly oiled 7x11 baking pan. When all peppers are stuffed and in the dish, pour the can of tomato sauce over the top. Cover with aluminum foil, and bake at 350°F for 30 minutes. Serves 4.

NOTES: Red peppers are wonderful in this recipe, but I generally use whatever is cheapest. Brown rice is my favorite in this recipe, but you can substitute others. If you use a skinny white rice, you may want to add slightly more than 2 cups. If you like a little more spice, add up to 2 tsps each of cumin and chili powder. To reduce fat content, steam the chopped onion and diced celery, and add the spices when mixing with the rice and beans.

CREOLE SQUASH & RICE

6 cups of winter squash

1 tsp basil

1 to 2 TBLS olive oil

1 green pepper, seeded and diced

1 onion, diced

2 or 3 cloves of garlic, minced

2 TBLS flour

1 15 oz can of tomatoes

1 8 oz can of tomato sauce

1 tsp salt

1 tsp parsley

1 bay leaf

1/4 tsp thyme

pinch of cayenne pepper

1 TBLS sweetener

basmati rice, cooked

◆ Peel the squash, cut in sections, and discard the seeds. Cut into cubes and place in a lightly greased casserole dish..

◆ Sauté the green pepper, onion, and garlic in olive oil, until the onion is just tender. Stir in the flour.

◆ Chop the can of tomatoes. Add tomatoes and tomato sauce to the pepper and onion mixture. Add remainder of seasonings. Simmer until the sauce is thickened. Pour over the squash.

◆ Cover the casserole dish, and bake at 350° F for 60 minutes. Serve with or over basmati rice. Serves 4 to 6.

NOTES: Hubbard squash is fairly easy to peel with a potato peeler. If you have no patience for peeling, make sure you stay away from acorn squash! I usually throw the can of tomatoes and tomato sauce in the blender, and end up with more of a puree than chopped tomatoes. For sweetener, consider using honey or maple syrup as a substitute for sugar.

VEGETABLE & PASTA TOSS

1/2 lb rotini spirals, cooked al dente

2 smallish-medium green peppers or 1 large

1 or 2 yellow squash

1 TBLS olive oil

1/4 cup water

3 cloves garlic, minced

2 cups mushrooms, quartered

16 oz can of white beans, with juice

2 tsp thyme

1/4 tsp rosemary

1 tsp basil

2 red peppers, roasted and diced (see PAGE 29)

◆ Prepare pasta according to label directions. Drain and set aside.

◆ Cut the green peppers in half lengthwise. Remove seeds and membranes. Now cut the peppers in half widthwise, and cut each quarter section into thin strips, yielding about 2 cups of strips. Slice the yellow squash into 1/4 inch slices, and then cut the slices into quarters.

◆ Place oil, water, and garlic in large skillet or shallow pot over medium heat. When the garlic has sizzled a few seconds, add the green pepper strips, mushrooms, and squash. Sauté 5 to 10 minutes, until the green peppers and squash are just tender.

◆ Add the can of beans with juice, red peppers, and spices. Mix well. Stir in pasta, until well coated. Simmer, covered, just until warm throughout. Serves 6.

NOTES: Vary the amounts of green pepper, mushrooms, and yellow squash depending on your tastes. Since anything edible in my kitchen gets eaten, I coarsely chop the mushroom stems and throw those in too. Finally, I've noticed that any leftovers never get re-heated because I eat it as a pasta salad the next day.

CHILI

3 TBLS olive oil

4 large onions, chopped

1 large green pepper, seeded, chopped

1 TBLS mustard seed

2 TBLS chili powder

2 tsp cumin seeds

1/2 tsp ground cinnamon

2 tsps unsweetened cocoa

3 16 oz cans of kidney beans, with juice

1 6 oz can of tomato paste

1 cup water

1 16 oz can of whole tomatoes

1 lb firm tofu, diced (see PAGE 52) (optional)

◆ In a large kettle, sauté onions and pepper in oil over medium high heat until onions are golden. Add mustard seeds, and cook, stirring, for another minute.

◆ Add chili powder, cumin, cocoa, cinnamon, beans and their juice, tomato paste, and water. Pour in the liquid from the can of tomatoes, then chop tomatoes and add to the pot (or pulse the tomatoes and their liquid in a blender). Add tofu, and stir.

◆ Reduce heat and simmer for 40 minutes, stirring often.

◆ After 20 minutes, check the consistency of your chili.   If the chili is runnier than you like, simmer uncovered. If the chili is thicker than you like, add more water and simmer covered. If the chili is just right, simmer covered. In any case, stir frequently to prevent scorching. Salt to taste.

◆ Serve with relishes of grated cheddar cheese, diced green onions, chopped tomatoes, diced green chilies, or peeled and diced cucumber. For vegans and non-dairy vegetarians, you can get a soy cheese (a non-dairy product, found in the dairy section at health food stores) if you want. Serves 4 to 6.

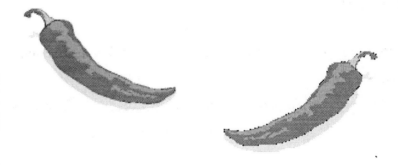

EGGPLANT LASAGNA

16 lasagna noodles

1 medium to large eggplant (about 1 pound)

1/4 lb mushrooms

2 small to medium zucchini

2 TBLS Olive oil

1 large onion,chopped

3 cloves garlic, minced

1 16 oz can of whole tomatoes, chopped

1 8 oz can of tomato sauce

1/2 tsp each paprika and pepper

1 tsp each basil and salt

2 tsp oregano

TOFU FILLING (see below)

fresh spinach

◆ Prepare lasagna noodles according to package directions. Set aside.

◆ Trim ends of unpeeled eggplant and dice. Thinly slice mushroom caps, and coarsely chop the stems. Julienne cut the zucchini.

◆ Heat oil in large kettle over medium heat. Add onion, garlic, eggplant, zucchini, and mushrooms. Sauté for 10 to 15 minutes, stirring constantly until onion is golden and zucchini is tender. Add tomatoes, tomato sauce, basil, oregano, salt, and pepper. Bring to a boil, then reduce heat, cover, and simmer for 30 minutes. Simmer longer uncovered for a thicker sauce. Remove from heat. Set aside 1/2 cup of sauce.

◆ **TOFU FILLING:** In a blender or food processor, place 1 lb of firm tofu, 1/4 cup lemon juice, 1/2 tsp ground nutmeg and 2 tsp honey. Process to a fine texture, like ricotta cheese.

◆ In a lightly oiled 9 by 13 pan, place a thin coating of vegetable sauce. Make three layers of the following: noodles, 1/4 tofu mixture, 1/3 vegetable sauce, covering of spinach leaves. After the third layer of spinach leaves, place the last of the noodles. Cover with remaining tofu mixture, and then with the half cup of sauce. Cover pan with foil, and bake for 45 minutes in 350° F oven. Let set for a couple minutes before cutting. Serves 12.

NOTES: If your guests are dairy eaters, substitute 1 lb ricotta or cottage cheese for the tofu mixture. The vegetable filling is pretty substantial, but if you want more cheesy stuff, use 1 1/2 lbs tofu or ricotta cheese, or add additional grated soy cheese or parmesan to the layers.. To jazz up the top, place a half cup of walnuts in a frying pan, and heat until brown, crisp, and fragrant. Coarsely chop and sprinkle on the final layer.

RICE NOODLE STIR FRY

1/2 package rice noodles

12 button mushrooms

1 medium zucchini

2 cups napa cabbage or bok choy, sliced

1 TBLS sesame oil

2 TBLS tamari sauce

1 TBLS cooking sherry

◆ Holding over a large bowl, open rice noodles package, and break into bit size pieces. Prepare rice noodles according to package directions. Drain and set aside.

◆ Cut mushrooms into quarters or sixths. Cut zucchini into quarter inch slices, and then cut each slice into halves.

◆ Heat sesame oil over medium low heat in a large frying pan or 3 quart pan.

◆Add mushrooms, stir to coat with oil, cover, and sauté for 2 minutes.

◆ Add zucchini, and cover, cooking for an additional 2 minutes until it turns slightly yellow.

◆ Add cabbage or bok choy, tamari sauce, and cooking sherry. Sauté until cabbage is tender.

◆ Add cooked rice noodles, and continue cooking until rice noodles are heated throughout. Serves 4 to 6.

NOTES: I prefer the bok choy in this recipe, but it may be a somewhat strong taste for the uninitiated palate. Chinese cabbage works well as a substitute. If you're not quite adventurous enough for either of these, try spinach as the last resort. The sesame oil is wonderful! If you absolutely must substitute for it, use olive oil, one clove of minced garlic, and 1/2 teaspoon of freshly shredded ginger. I break up the rice noodles before cooking because I find it easier than chopping the cooked ones.

NO MEAT LOAF

1 small onion

1 lb firm tofu

1/2 cup wheat germ

1/2 cup oat crumbs (see PAGE 29)

1/3 cup fresh parsley, chopped

1/3 cup soy or rice milk

3 TBLS tamari sauce

1/8 tsp black pepper

1/4 tsp oregano

1/4 tsp garlic granules

1/2 tsp thyme

1 heaping teaspoon dijon mustard

◆ In the food processor, chop the onion into small pieces. Add the drained tofu, and chop until it is also broken up. Place mixture into a separate bowl.

◆ Add remaining ingredients. Mix, either by hand or spoon. For best flavoring, cover with plastic and let sit for an hour.

◆ Press into oiled loaf pan. Bake in 350° F oven for 45 to 60 minutes. The loaf will be browned on top and pulling away from the sides of the pan when done. Let cool for 10 minutes before turning onto serving platter. Serves 6 to 8.

NOTES: Letting sit before baking is not essential. Because tofu picks up the flavors of the foods it's combined with, I prefer to make this dish ahead of time, and let all the ingredients get to know each other well.

HOW TO SUBSTITUTE

Here are a few guidelines on how to adapt some of your favorite and proven recipes to vegetarian guidelines.

CHANGE....   **TO....**

butter, lard   canola margarine
                        corn oil margarine
                        vegetable oil (use 80%
                                of amount called for)

beef or
 chicken stock   vegetable broth

sugar   honey (use half the amount
                                called for)
                        maple syrup
                        molasses
                        fructose

milk   soy milk
                        rice milk
                          (soy & rice milk will not
                            work with instant pudding
                            mixes)

eggs in baking   1/2 banana
                        1/4 cup tofu

gelatin   1 TBLS granulated agar-agar
                        2 TBLS flaked agar-agar

SIDE DISHES

NOTES:

Many of you undoubtedly already have favorite ways of fixing vegetables. Here are just a few ways to try something different, yet are easy to prepare.

DIJON CABBAGE

1 TBLS olive oil

6 cups green cabbage (one small head), sliced

3 carrots, thinly sliced

1/4 cup green onions, sliced

1 TBLS Dijon mustard

2 tsp apple cider vinegar

2 tsp brown sugar

1/2 tsp salt

1/3 cup walnuts, coarsely chopped

◆ Heat oil in a large skillet, and sauté cabbage, carrots, and green onions for 10 to 15 minutes, until the cabbage is crisp tender. Stir frequently.

◆ Mix together mustard, vinegar, brown sugar, and salt.

◆ Add mustard mixture and walnuts to cabbage. Toss well, and cook for up to 5 more minutes, stirring constantly. Serves 4.

HOT ANTIPASTO VEGGIES

1/4 cup Italian salad dressing

1 clove garlic, minced

2 green onions, chopped

1 small head of cauliflower, cut into flowerettes (about 3 cups)

1/4 cup water

1 medium zucchini, halved, and cut into 1/4 inch slices

1/4 tsp basil

6 black olives, sliced (optional)

2 TBLS green pepper, chopped (optional)

1 cup cherry tomatoes, halved (optional)

◆ In a 2 quart saucepan, sauté onion and garlic in salad dressing, for 2 minutes. Add cauliflower and water. Cover and cook over low heat for 10 minutes.

◆ Add zucchini, basil, olives, and peppers. Cook an additional 5 minutes, until zucchini is yellowed and cauliflower is tender. Add tomatoes and heat through. Salt and pepper to taste. Serves 4.

NOTES: If you're using a low-fat water based Italian dressing, double the quantity to 1/2 cup, or add an additional 1/4 of water to the dressing.

YAM CHIPS

2 yams, scrubbed, cut into 1/4 inch slices

2 TBLS olive oil

1 tsp seasoning salt

1/2 tsp paprika

1/4 tsp nutmeg

◆ Preheat oven to 425° F.

◆ Scrub the yams under warm water, and cut into 1/4 inch slices.

◆ Mix together seasoning salt, paprika, and nutmeg.

◆ Pour olive oil onto a cookie sheet, and coat evenly. Place yam slices on single layer of the cookie sheet. Sprinkle half of the seasoning mixture on the yams.

◆ Turn the yams slices over, so that both sides are now oiled. Sprinkle remaining seasoning mixture over yam slices.

◆ Bake for 10 minutes. Turn slices, and bake an additional 10 minutes. Serves 4.

POTATO WEDGES

2 to 3 russet potatoes

2 TBLS olive oil

Seasoning: Herbs du Provence

    or   Cajun Spices

    or   a mixture of your own creation

◆   Preheat oven to 400° F.

◆   Scrub potatoes clean, under warm water. Cut lengthwise into 1/2 inch wedges.

◆   Pour olive oil on a cookie sheet, and spread evenly. Coat the potato wedges with olive oil by turning the wedge on all three sides while placing on the cookie sheet. Sprinkle with seasoning. Cover with aluminum foil. Bake for 30 to 45 minutes, until potatoes are tender when stabbed with a fork. Remove foil. Bake an additional 15 to 20 minutes, to create a crusty outer edge. Serves 4.

ZUCCHINI & EGGPLANT

1 16 oz can of whole tomatoes

1 tsp basil

1 TBLS oregano

1 tsp honey

2 tsp olive oil

2 tsp tamari sauce

2 zucchini

1 medium eggplant, peeled

1/2 tsp salt

1/8 tsp black pepper

◆ Place canned tomatoes, basil, oregano, and honey in a food processor or blender. Coarsely chop, and set aside.

◆ Cut zucchini into 1/4 or 1/2 inch slices. Dice eggplant into 1/4 or 1/2 inch cubes. In large pot over medium heat, stir zucchini and eggplant in oil and tamari sauce until well coated. Reduce heat slightly, cover, and cook until crisp tender, checking and stirring frequently. Add tomato mixture, and cook for 10 more minutes. Serves 4.

GINGER CARROTS

8 medium carrots, peeled

1 TBLS brown sugar

1 tsp cornstarch

1/4 tsp ground ginger

1/2 cup orange juice

1 TBLS canola margarine

◆ Slice carrots 1/4 to 1/2 inch thick. For variety, slice on the bias. Cook in saucepan containing 1 inch of boiling salted water until tender (10 to 20 minutes, depending upon thickness).

◆ In small saucepan over medium high heat, combine brown sugar, cornstarch, ginger, and a dash of salt. Add orange juice, and cook, stirring constantly until thickened. Boil 1 minute. Remove from heat, and stir in margarine. Pour hot mixture over hot carrots, and toss to coat. Serves 6.

BROWN RICE

1 cup brown rice

2 cups water

1 cup vegetable broth

◆ Place all items in a rice cooker, and push the 'on' button. If you don't have a rice cooker, you have my sympathies. I value mine even more than the food processor.

◆ Otherwise, place 2 cups of water and 1 cup vegetable broth in a saucepan. Bring to a boil. Add rice, cover, reduce heat, and simmer for 40 minutes, until the liquid is absorbed. Do not stir. Serves 2 to 4.

NOTES: When cooking rice, err on the side of too much water. It can always be drained out. Using vegetable broth in cooking gives more flavor to rice, especially if it is being served on the side as is. If you wish, you may use a total of 3 cups of water and no vegetable broth. Increase proportions of rice, water, and broth to increase the amount of servings.

RICE NOODLES

1 package rice noodles

1 to 2 TBLS tamari sauce

◆ Break up noodles first if you prefer shorter pieces. Add to boiling water. Simmer for 10 minutes, or cover, remove from heat, and let sit for 10 minutes.

◆ Drain noodles. Mix with tamari sauce to coat, and serve. Serves 4 to 6.

STIR FRY COMBOS

Stir frying means quickly cooking vegetables in a minimal amount of liquid.   It can be done in a wok or large frying pan.   The advantages are fast cooking time and crisp, flavorful vegetables.   On the negative side, your time is spent chopping before hand.   This is an experimental activity, so try variations until you find ones you like.

STEP 1: PREPARE VEGETABLES

Cut, slice, dice, cube, or whatever, the vegetables you wish to use.   Prepare 1/2 cup of vegetable broth with boiling water and 1/2 tsp vegetable bouillon.   Set flavorings (see Step 4) to be used by the stovetop.   Once cooking starts, you need to stay by the stove.

STEP 2: HEAT LIQUID

Place into frying pan or wok over medium heat one of the following:

- ◆ 1 to 2 TBLS sesame oil
- ◆ 2 TBLS olive oil, with 1 clove minced garlic and
       1/4 tsp grated fresh ginger
- ◆ 1/4 cup vegetable broth with 1 TBLS tamari sauce

STEP 3: ADD VEGETABLES

Stir frequently, almost constantly.

Not all vegetables get added at once.   LONGER COOKING vegetables go first, followed by SHORTER COOKING vegetables, followed by HEAT THROUGHS.

LONGER COOKING

(slice thinly, and if possible, on the bias)

celery	carrots	cabbage
mushrooms	green onions	fresh snow peas
broccoli	cauliflower	

and any SHORTER COOKING vegetable in thick slices or chunks

SHORTER COOKING

zucchini	yellow squash	bok choy
frozen snow peas	spinach	chinese cabbage

HEAT THROUGHS

bean sprouts	water chestnuts	bamboo shoots
canned mushrooms	baby corn	pineapple
walnuts	almonds	cashews

STEP 4: ADDITIONS WHILE COOKING

While stirring with one hand, the other hand may want to add additional liquids or flavorings. Add flavorings first. If extra liquid is still needed to prevent scorching or sticking, use vegetable broth. Flavorings include:

> tamari sauce
>
> soy sauce
>
> cooking sherry
>
> cooking wine
>
> hoisin sauce
>
> vegetable broth
>
> pineapple juice
>
> orange juice

If you're just starting to experiment, try 2 TBLS tamari sauce with 1 TBLS cooking sherry.

COMBINATIONS TO TRY

mushrooms, yellow squash, spinach

snow peas, green onions, water chestnuts

green onions, celery, cauliflower, mushrooms

mushrooms, bok choy, bean sprouts

carrots, broccoli, mushrooms, walnut halves

bean sprouts, baby corn, mushrooms, chinese cabbage

red pepper, snow peas, cubed tofu

HOLIDAYS

Thanksgiving or Christmas

Fourth of July

NOTES:

Holidays can be somewhat trying times for cooking vegetarian in a non-vegetarian kitchen. Many holiday traditions are centered around food, so hopefully here are a few new traditions you can start in your kitchen.

MUSHROOM ROAST

2 TBLS olive oil

1 large onion, chopped

1 lb mushrooms, finely chopped

2 TBLS whole wheat flour

1/2 cup ground almonds

1 1/4 cup oat crumbs (see PAGE 29)

1 tsp Herbs du Provence (see NOTES below)

1/4 tsp salt

whole almonds and parsley to garnish

◆ Sauté onion for 5 minutes in olive oil. Add mushrooms, and sauté an additional 5 minutes. Remove from heat. Stir in flour, almonds, 1 cup oat crumbs, herbs, and salt.

◆ Lightly grease (or rub with olive oil) a loaf tin or small casserole dish. Line the bottom with 1/4 cup oat crumbs. Place mushroom mixture in dish. Bake 1 hour at 350° F.

◆ To serve, turn loaf upside down on serving platter. Garnish with whole almonds and parsley. Serves 4.

NOTES: This is a special treat that can share space in the oven with the holiday turkey or ham. (I'm assuming that some of the salads and side dishes are already prepared vegetarian.) If you don't have Herbs du Provence, substitute 1/4 tsp each of oregano, basil, thyme, and sage.

BASIC GRAVY

1/4 cup olive oil

1/2 cup whole wheat flour

2 cups vegetable broth

1/4 cup tamari sauce

salt, pepper

◆ In a frying pan or large bottom saucepan, heat oil. Stir in flour, cooking and stirring constantly for a few minutes. Stir in vegetable broth, SLOWLY to avoid lumping. When well blended, add tamari sauce. Cook over low heat, stirring constantly, until thickened, about 10 minutes. Add salt and pepper to taste. Makes about 2 cups.

MUSHROOM GRAVY

2 TBLS olive oil

1 small onion, finely chopped

1 clove garlic, minced

1 cup sliced mushrooms

2 TBLS whole wheat flour

1 1/2 cups vegetable broth

salt, pepper

◆ Heat oil in frying pan or large bottom saucepan. Sauté onion and garlic for 3 to 4 minutes, until soft. Add mushrooms. Sauté an additional 2 to 3 minutes, stirring. Stir in flour. SLOWLY add vegetable broth, stirring constantly. Simmer, stirring constantly, until thickened. Add more broth if gravy gets too thick. Add salt and pepper to taste. Makes about 1 1/4 cups.

MASHED POTATOES

6 potatoes

water

1/2 tsp salt

1 bay leaf

1 celery stalk, with leaves

3 TBLS canola margarine

1/3 cup of soy or rice milk

◆ Cut potatoes into quarters (oh, go ahead, leave the skins on!). Place in a large pot, and cover with water. Add salt, bay leaf, and celery stalk. Bring to a boil, then cover and simmer until potatoes are done.

◆ Drain. Remove bay leaf and celery stalk. Add margarine and soy milk to potatoes, and mash. Adjust amount of soy milk to get the consistency you desire. Season to taste with pepper and/or 2 TBLS fresh chopped parsley. Serves 6 to 8.

CANDIED YAMS

5 medium sized yams or sweet potatoes, scrubbed or peeled

Salt

Paprika

1/3 cup maple syrup

1/8 tsp ginger

dash of nutmeg

2 TBLS chopped pecans

2 TBLS canola margarine

◆ Cook whole yams in boiling water until tender. Drain, and cut into half inch slices.

◆ Place in a shallow oiled baking dish. Sprinkle on salt, paprika, maple syrup, ginger, nutmeg and pecans. For more sweetness, increase maple syrup to 1/2 cup. Dot the top with margarine.

◆ Bake uncovered in 375° F oven for about 20 minutes, until glazed. Serves 4 to 6.

PUMPKIN PIE

This recipe comes in 3 parts: Pie Crust, Filling, and Whipped Topping.

Pie Crust

> 1 1/2 cup whole wheat flour
>
> 1/4 tsp salt
>
> 1/4 cup canola oil
>
> 1/4 cup soy or rice milk, or water

◆ Combine ingredients into dough. Add more milk or water if dough is too dry. Roll out on floured surface. Place in 9" pie tin, trimming excess from edge, and folding under the top 1/2 inch to form crust edge. Set aside.

Filling

1 16 oz can of cooked pumpkin

1 cup soy or rice milk

3/4 cup brown sugar

1/4 cup cornstarch

1/4 cup oil

2 tsp cinnamon

1/2 tsp each ginger and mace

1/4 tsp each nutmeg, allspice, and salt

◆ Preheat oven to 425° F.

◆ Combine everything in the food processor, and blend until smooth. For a variation in sweetener, change the 3/4 cup brown sugar to 1/4 cup maple syrup and 1/2 cup brown sugar. Pour into pie crust..

◆ Place pie in oven. After 5 minutes, reduce oven heat to 325°F. Bake an hour, until knife inserted in pie filling comes out clean. If the crust is getting too brown too quickly, loosely cover pie crust edges with aluminum foil, and continue baking until filling is set.

Whipped topping

1 10 oz package of silken tofu

1/4 cup canola oil

1/4 cup confectioner's sugar or fructose

1 tsp vanilla

1/8 tsp salt

1 tsp lemon juice

dash of cinnamon

◆ Combine in blender until smooth. Refrigerate.

NOTES: This topping does not mound in the same way as dairy whipped toppings, so you'll probably use less of it per serving. Adjust seasonings to your taste. Try substituting 1/4 tsp almond extract in place of the vanilla.

TOFU BURGERS

1 lb firm tofu

1/4 cup wheat germ

1/4 cup whole wheat flour

1 TBLS grated onion

1/2 tsp each basil, oregano, and ground cumin

1 tsp tamari sauce

◆ Mix all ingredients together in food processor. Form into 4 or 6 patties.

◆ Cook using one of the following three methods:

    1) Place the patties on a piece of aluminum foil, and cook on the barbecue grill.

    2) Fry in a tablespoon of olive oil on the stove.

    3) Bake in a 350° F oven on a lightly oiled cookie sheet until browned, about 30 minutes (turn once while cooking).

Serves 4 to 6.

OAT BURGERS

4 TBLS olive oil

1 medium potato, grated

1 medium onion, grated

1/2 cup walnuts, ground

1 cup cooked oatmeal

1 cup oat crumbs (see PAGE 29)

1/2 tsp salt

1/2 tsp sage

2 TBLS tamari sauce

◆ Sauté potato, onion, and nuts in olive oil until soft. Add remaining ingredients and mix thoroughly. Form into 6 patties.

◆ Cook using one of the following three methods:
> 1) Place the patties on a piece of aluminum foil, and cook on the barbecue grill.
> 2) Fry in a tablespoon of olive oil on the stove.
> 3) Bake in a 350° F oven on a lightly oiled cookie sheet until browned, about 30 minutes (turn once while cooking).

Serves 6.

VEGGIE KEBABS

1 large red onion, cut in 1/2 inch wedges

2 red bell peppers, cut in 1 inch wedges

12 mushrooms

1 large zucchini, cut in 1/2 inch slices

1 pound firm tofu, frozen and thawed;

   cut into 1 inch or larger cubes (see PAGE 52)

1 cup marinade (see NOTES below)

1/4 cup olive oil

◆ Place the above in a glass baking dish. Pour on the marinade, mix to coat, and let sit for 1 to 3 hours. Refrigerate if longer than 3 hours.

◆ Thread vegetables and tofu onto skewers. Combine olive oil with 1/2 cup of marinade. Brush onto skewered vegetables. Place skewers on grill, turning until lightly browned, brushing as often as desired. Serves 4.

NOTES: This recipe can share grill space with the hamburgers and steaks.   Options for marinades, besides your own personal favorite, include teriyaki sauce, a vinaigrette dressing, or salad dressing, made without oil.   My personal favorite is an oriental sesame salad dressing mix made by Good Seasoning. Do not use oil in the marinade, as that will prevent the tofu from absorbing the flavors.

THE HOUSE GUEST

Yes, they're staying for several days, the whole vegetarian lot of them. Here's a few suggestions on making the stay easier:

✦ Stock the kitchen with a few basics, as listed on PAGE 28 .

✦ Ask the guests in advance what they would like to have on hand for breakfasts and snacks.

✦ Get a gift certificate to a local health food store, and send the guest there on the first day to stock up on supplies.

✦ Find out how particular the vegetarians are. Complete the chart on PAGE 19.

✦ Ask the guest if he or she would like to prepare a meal for you as a means of introducing you to vegetarian cooking. (Hey, if your guest were coming from Ghana for instance, you probably wouldn't hesitate to have a typical Ghanaian meal prepared for you.)

✦ Cook more than needed for dinner, so that there are leftovers for lunch or easy suppers.

✦ Plan potluck or buffet-style meals. Makes it easier for you to eat that fried chicken while your guest is having brown rice.

✦ Keep in mind that the deviations in your diet are temporary. You might even try for a positive experience in using the vegetarian's expertise in improving your vegetarian cooking.

DID YOU KNOW...

... one red or yellow bell pepper has 4 times the amount of vitamin C as a single orange. A green pepper only has twice the vitamin C content of an orange.

... an almond is not a nut. An almond is the pit of a fruit called a drupe, similar to a peach.

... the apple tree is a member of the rose family. While the rose blossom is more fragrant than its cousin the apple blossom,   you'll probably enjoy eating the apple more than the rosehip.

... the Indians in the Andes Mountains of South America cultivated potatoes for 4000 years, developing about 3,000 varieties.   They also developed the first freeze-dried process for potatoes.   And you thought instant potatoes were the results of modern technology!

... corn has been cultivated for so many thousands of years that it can no longer grow in the wild.

NUTRITION STUFF

A lot of misconceptions exist concerning how healthy a vegetarian diet is, especially among mothers of growing boys and Americans raised on the "Four Food Groups" diagrams of the 1950s and later. So perhaps out of self-defense as much as anything else, vegetarians tend to be pretty knowledgeable about nutrition.

Nutrition is the process by which plants, animals, and people take in and utilize food material, the food material that provides the fuel for living. The body is satisfied as long as it's getting the right fuel in sufficient quantity. Insufficient nutrients in any sort of diet can lead to the body continuing to eat and eat, in search of the needed elements. Bottom line, it's not quantity of food but content.

In the area of basics, many people believe that meat and dairy products are the primary, if not only, sources of protein, iron, and calcium. Not true! Here's just a brief lesson.

PROTEIN

The World Health Organization's guidelines are 40 grams of protein a day, which should be no more than 10% of calories consumed. Professional nutritionists recognize that a vegetarian eating a varied diet almost never suffers from protein deficiency. Meat-eaters should be careful -- too much protein can lead to progressive kidney disease as well as deplete the calcium stored in bones.

These foods are good sources of protein:

tofu	artichokes
soy milk	asparagus
pumpkin seeds	bamboo shoots
lentils	beet greens
lima beans	red cabbage
garbanzo beans	cauliflower
pinto beans	chives
red beans	wheat germ
white beans	black walnuts
split peas	rice
bean sprouts	oats

IRON

The RDA of iron for men and post-menopausal women is 10 mg a day, with 15 mg a day recommended for women of childbearing years. Like many nutrients, it's not just the sheer numbers of milligrams to absorb, but also source and combination with other nutrients. Iron, for instance, needs the help of vitamin C to be absorbed. Which means that eating 2 mg of iron accompanied by vitamin C may be more readily absorbed into the body than 5 mg of iron alone. Be aware that once iron is consumed, it stays in the body unless released by bleeding. Too much iron has been connected to tissue damage, heart disease, cancer, and premature aging.

These foods are good sources of iron:

brown rice	split peas
wheat bran	dried apricots
wheat germ	walnuts
lima beans	almonds
mung beans	tofu
pinto beans	blackstrap molasses
red beans	spinach
white beans	sesame seeds
lentils	sunflower seeds
soybeans	

CALCIUM

Adults need about 800 mg of calcium a day, according to the RDA, but 500 mg a day is sufficient per the World Health Organization, especially if you do not eat meat. Children need more, since 90% of the body's calcium absorption occurs before adulthood. If you're feeding a vegetarian child or teen on a regular basis, there are vegetarian cookbooks and nutrition guides geared to kids. Get one. Otherwise, don't worry about it.

Calcium occurs in nuts, seeds, vegetables, rice, and legumes. Once again, simply having a varied diet will satisfy requirements. By the way, bone density is regulated by hormones, not calcium. Scientific studies have shown there is no relationship between bone density and calcium intake. If you're drinking milk to try to prevent osteoporosis, think again. The animal protein in the milk is most likely sucking the calcium from your body as fast as, or faster than, your body can make use of the calcium in the milk.

These foods are good sources of calcium:

almonds	soybeans
beet greens	black turtle beans
broccoli	wax beans
seaweed	white beans
yellow squash	dried figs
zucchini	raisins
sunflower seeds	celery
tofu	onions
brown rice	sweet potato
lima beans	chickpeas
navy beans	kidney beans
pinto beans	collards

THE NEW FOOD PYRAMID

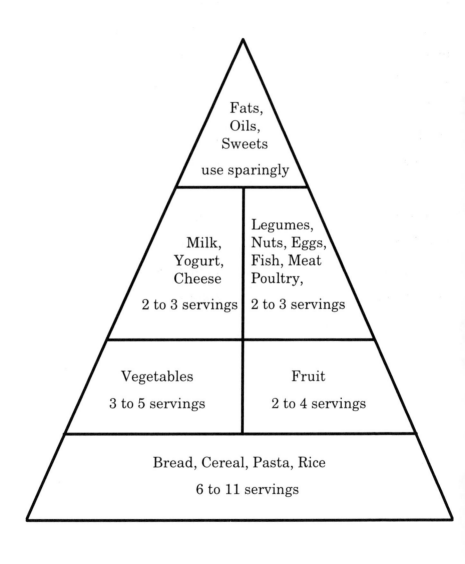

Fats,
Oils,
Sweets

use sparingly

Milk,
Yogurt,
Cheese

2 to 3 servings

Legumes,
Nuts, Eggs,
Fish, Meat
Poultry,

2 to 3 servings

Vegetables

3 to 5 servings

Fruit

2 to 4 servings

Bread, Cereal, Pasta, Rice

6 to 11 servings

SAMPLE MENUS

Here are a few suggestions on mixing and matching the recipes in this cookbook, along with some of your own favorites.

A few ideas to keep in mind are:

✦ For a well-rounded meal, serve at least 1 grain (rice, pasta) or 1 legume (dried beans, nuts, tofu), and 2 vegetables (in salad or side dish).

✦ Blend flavors. Try not to put the exact same seasonings on every dish. However, be aware that extremes in seasonings between dishes is confusing to the tastebuds. For example, a heavy ginger flavor on vegetables does not blend well with a heavy oregano flavor of lasagne.

✦ Have a variety of textures. For instance, a few pecans added to the candied yams creates a bit of a crunch in an otherwise relatively 'soft' dish.

LUNCH, LIGHT SUPPERS

The Other Bean Salad

Aztec Soup

Cornbread

Green Salad

Stuffed Peppers

Hot, crusty bread

Lentil & Rice Salad

White Bean & Garlic Chowder

Hot Crusty Bread

Earth Salad

Chili

Cornbread

Raw vegetables

Rice Noodle Stir Fry

DINNERS

Fresh Slaw

Stir Fried Vegetables

Brown Rice or Rice Noodles

Marinated Slaw

Veggie Burgers with Gravy

Potato Wedges

Rice Noodle Stir Fry

Ginger Carrots

No Meat Loaf

Salad

Carrot Rice Loaf

Eggplant & Zucchini Combo

Earth Salad

Steamed Vegetables

Brown Rice

THE HALF FULL VIEW

(A list of ingredients used in this cookbook.)

Grains
lasagna noodles
oats
rice, basmati
rice, brown
rice, white
rice noodles
rotini spirals
wheat germ
whole wheat flour

Legumes
black turtle beans
kidney beans
pinto beans
red lentils
tofu
white navy beans

Liquids
juice, lemon
juice, orange
juice, pineapple
milk, almond
milk, rice
milk, soy
vegetable stock or broth

Miscellaneous
cheese
cooking sherry
cornstarch
hoisin sauce
margarine, canola
margarine, corn oil
margarine, vegetable
mustard, dijon
mustard, prepared
oil, canola
oil, olive
oil, vegetable
olives, black
olives, green
tamari sauce
tortilla chips
vinegar, balsamic
vinegar, cider
vinegar, red wine
vinegar, white

Nuts & Seeds
almonds
cashews
pecans
pine nuts
pumpkin seeds
sunflower seeds
walnuts

Spices, Herbs, & Seasonings
allspice
basil
bay leaf
black pepper
bouquet garni
brown sugar
cayenne pepper
chives
chili powder
cilantro
cinnamon
cloves, ground
cocoa, unsweetened
cumin, ground
cumin seed
dill weed
garlic, cloves
garlic, granules
garlic, powder
ginger, fresh
ginger, ground
Herbs du Provence
lemon
mace
mustard, dry
mustard seed
nutmeg
oregano
paprika
parsley
rosemary
sage
salt
thyme

Sweeteners
fructose
honey
maple syrup
sugar, brown
sugar, white

Vegetables
avocado
bean sprouts
beets
beet greens
broccoli
cabbage, chinese or napa
cabbage, green
cabbage, red
carrots
cauliflower
celeriac root
celery
corn, baby
corn, frozen
cucumber
eggplant
mushrooms
onions
onion, green
onion, Vidalia
parsnip
peas, snow (or peapods)
pepper, green bell
pepper, green chili
pepper, red bell
pepper, yellow bell

Vegetables (continued)

potato	tomato paste
pumpkin, canned	tomato sauce
spinach	turnip
squash, butternut	water chestnuts
squash, hubbard	yams
squash, yellow	zucchini
tomatoes, canned	

MORE HELP

Possibly, just possibly, you've decided vegetarian cooking is something you may want to do on a more frequent basis. If so, here are a few suggestions.

MAGAZINES

VEGETARIAN TIMES, P.O. Box 570, Oak Park, IL 60303

VEGGIE LIFE, EGW Publishing Co., 1041 Shary Circle, Concord, CA 94518

BOOKS

THE AMERICAN VEGETARIAN COOKBOOK -- From the Fit for Life Kitchen, by Marilyn Diamond. Warner Books, Inc., 1990.

A CELEBRATION OF WELLNESS, by James Levin, M.D. and Natalie Cederquist. GLO, Inc., 1992.

ECOLOGICAL COOKING -- Recipes to Save the Planet, by Joanne Stepanik and Kathy Hecker. The Book Publishing Company, 1991.

FOOD FOR LIFE -- How the New Four Food Groups Can Save Your Life, by Neal Barnard, M.D. Harmony Book, 1993.

SUNSET MENUS AND RECIPES FOR VEGETARIAN COOKING, by the Editors of Sunset Books and Sunset Magazine. Lane Publishing Co., 1981.

NOTES:

If you're going to buy a vegetarian cookbook, do a little thinking ahead of time. There's a wide variety of cookbooks that fall into the vegetarian category. What sort of additional information do you want besides recipes? Nutrition? Product explanations? Do you want a cookbook that uses dairy and eggs?

Think of three or four recipes you'd be likely to make, such as pasta dishes, rice casseroles, bean salad, or baked desserts. Flip through the cookbook looking at these particular recipes. Are they using ingredients you already have or are willing to buy? Do the instructions seem more complicated than you're willing to spend time following? If you're concerned about dairy, do recipes call for soy milk or milk (the two are not always interchangeable)?

Taking a little extra time at the bookstore reading recipes will lessen disappointments in the kitchen!

ADVICE FROM THE

Use these pages to record the helpful
hints you find along the way.

VOICES OF EXPERIENCE

BIBLIOGRAPHY

THE AMERICAN VEGETARIAN COOKBOOK -- From the Fit for Life Kitchen, by Marilyn Diamond. Warner Books, Inc., 1990.

A CELEBRATION OF WELLNESS, by James Levin, M.D. and Natalie Cederquist. GLO, Inc., 1992.

COMPASSIONATE EATING: A Nutritional & Recipe Guide, by Kim Le, Ph.D. 1989.

ECOLOGICAL COOKING -- Recipes to Save the Planet, by Joanne Stepanik and Kathy Hecker. The Book Publishing Company, 1991.

FOOD FOR LIFE -- How the New Four Food Groups Can Save Your Life, by Neal Barnard, M.D. Harmony Book, 1993.

"How Many Vegetarians are there?", by Charles Stahler, THE VEGETARIAN JOURNAL, Vegetarian Resource Group, 1995.

THE GREAT FOOD ALMANAC: A Feast of Facts from A to Z, by Irena Chalmers. Collins, 1994.

SUNSET MENUS AND RECIPES FOR VEGETARIAN COOKING, by the Editors of Sunset Books and Sunset Magazine. Lane Publishing Co., 1981.

THE VEGAN DIET: True Vegetarian Cookery, by David Scott and Claire Golding. Rider, 1985.

If you are dissatisfied with this book, then please, **PLEASE** return it for a full refund.

On a separate sheet of paper, please print:

    1) your name, as payee on the refund check

    2) your address

    3) why you wish to return the book. Your criticisms would be most appreciated.

Mail the book and sheet of paper to:

    PLACIDLY AMID THE NOISE
    P.O. Box 16914
    Colorado Springs, CO   80935-6914

Allowing for postal transit times, you should receive your refund check in approximately three weeks.

COMING IN 1997!

THE

SUPERMARKET

VEGETARIAN

An easy vegetarian cookbook using only the ingredients found in supermarkets!

DESIGNED FOR:

✦ beginning vegetarians and vegetarian "wanna be's"

✦ the health conscious who want to reduce animal product consumption

✦ cooks who like good food but do not have the patience for complicated recipes with exotic ingredients

CHAPTERS INCLUDE:

✦ eating well without being a slave to nutrition

✦ introductions to food you may have never met

✦ more recipes, including desserts and snacks, and
adapting your favorite recipes

✦ convenience cooking with FRESH ingredients

If you wish to be informed when THE SUPERMARKET VEGETARIAN is available, send a card or letter with your name, address, and the words "SUPERMARKET VEGETARIAN" to:

PLACIDLY AMID THE NOISE

P.O. Box 16914

Colorado Springs, CO   80935-6914

Order form for:

HOW TO FEED A VEGETARIAN

Total

Quantity: _____   @ $12.95 each   _____

CO Residents, add 4% sales tax   _____

SHIPPING & HANDLING   _____
   $1.95 for the first book
   $ .95 for each additional book

ORDER TOTAL: _____

Please make check or money order payable to:
          PLACIDLY AMID THE NOISE

SHIP TO (please print):

Name _____

Address _____

City, State, Zip _____

Daytime phone: (   ) _____   Nighttime phone: (   ) _____

Mail to: PLACIDLY AMID THE NOISE
               Order Dept.
               P.O. Box 16914
               Colorado Springs, CO   80935-6914

Order form for:

HOW TO FEED A VEGETARIAN

Total

Quantity: _____ @ $12.95 each _____

CO Residents, add 4% sales tax _____

SHIPPING & HANDLING _____
$1.95 for the first book
$ .95 for each additional book

ORDER TOTAL: _____

Please make check or money order payable to:
PLACIDLY AMID THE NOISE

SHIP TO (please print):

Name _____

Address _____

City, State, Zip _____

Daytime phone: ( ) _____ Nighttime phone: ( ) _____

Mail to: PLACIDLY AMID THE NOISE
Order Dept.
P.O. Box 16914
Colorado Springs, CO 80935-6914